Gallery Books
Editor: Peter Fallon

THE GIRL WHO MARRIED
THE REINDEER

Eiléan Ní Chuilleanáin

THE GIRL
WHO MARRIED
THE REINDEER

Gallery Books

The Girl who Married the Reindeer
is first published
simultaneously in paperback
and in a clothbound edition
on 28 November 2001.

The Gallery Press
Loughcrew
Oldcastle
County Meath
Ireland

ISBN 1 85235 303 1 (*paperback*)
        1 85235 304 X (*clothbound*)

A CIP catalogue record for this book
is available from the British Library.

· The Gallery Press acknowledges the financial assistance of
An Chomhairle Ealaíon / The Arts Council, Ireland, and
the Arts Council of Northern Ireland.

Contents

THE GIRL WHO MARRIED
THE REINDEER

The Crossroads

I have been at the crossroads now
All the time without leaving
Since the afternoon of Shrove Tuesday.

They brought me the blessed ashes
Wrapped in tissue paper.

When I woke on Palm Sunday
The palm branches had been left
On the damp stones of the stile.

I heard them at Easter
Across the ploughed fields,

And the little girls came and stood
A little way off, to show me
Their embroidered dancing costumes.

Now it is a long time to the Feast of the Assumption,
When my mother will come

To collect me in her pony and trap
And we will go calling on all our cousins
And take tea and sherry in their parlours.

Anchoress

In the last season, she changed her ways.
The pilgrim would find only
The mossgrown window beside the church porch
And through it at times a loaf and water were passed.

A few words, a command. Yes she knew who was there,
She still prayed for them all by name. I remember
When she would give me an hour of her visions,
When she would levitate — she was always deaf —
When thin pipe music resounded beyond the grilles.

Sunday

I can't go there, but I know just how it will be.

The children will be running round and round
The house, landing to snatch a bite of food
While the couples are keeping time with knife and fork
At a table under the wisteria.

A long time later the young ones will have come to rest
In a wide half-circle which is complete
Because the ducks will also have come back
With two rows of ducklings and will be all
Coiling their necks to sleep under the terrace.

I have to hear the chestnut choir
Singing in the mountain convent. They won't remember
    me there,
But all the same, this autumn,
I am going to hear the office they sing on that Sunday
At vespers, before the longest vigil of the year.

The Chestnut Choir

All the way up the mountain
Boys were breaking branches of chestnuts.
The leaves scattered on the road.
When she stopped for a hot brandy
The bar was warm, the windows misted over,
A small girl, on her way to bed,
Her dolly under her elbow, crouched
Staring into the wood-stove's flaming centre.

Outside again, her steps crunched on frosted gravel,
The trees faded into mountainside,
And still it was not dark.

The convent was close at hand,
The chapel door half open.
She let herself in to a box pew at the back
And closed the latch. The voices had begun,
A long tutti wrapping
The walls in layers of sound.
The alto coasted and crawled,
The words were sharpened as the last light fell away:

Behold how wide are the doors
That open beneath the furnace
Where the flame dives under the stone . . .

She leaned her cheek against the wall and the sound
Came to join her, flinching in her teeth.
Then there was silence, and the two candle-flames
Flickered, reflected in wood. She knew
They were still there while she,
The wanderer, was free to be away.
The bar would be shut, and some beast
Was snuffling outside,
But she got up and left them to their vigil.

The Angel in the Stone

Trampled in the causeway, the stone the builders passed over
Calls out: 'Bone of the ranked heights, from darkness
Where moss and spiders never venture.
You know what ways I plumbed, past what hard threshold;

'You see our affliction, you know
How we were made and how we decay. At hand
When the backbone splintered in the sea tide, you have heard
The twang of the waves breaking our bones.

'You look down where the high peaks are ranging,
You see them flickering like flames —
They are like a midge dancing at evening.

'Give me rest for one long day of mourning;
Let me lie on the stone bench above the tree-line
And drink water for one whole day.'

The Cloister of Bones

I begin from the highest point,
Best of all a belltower.

I see the tops of heads, cobbles,
Terraces all scuttling down
As if they hunted something buried
Between ledges where tables are set in the morning,
Under plants that grow over walls and pergolas,
The slopes of sheds, the stashed pruning-shears,
Under the measured walk of cats.

I am searching for a shape, a den, watching
For the cloistering blank of a street wall,
A dark reticence of windows
Banked over an inner court,
Especially rooves, arched and bouncing
Naves; a corseted apse,
And always, even if the chapel sinks
Deep inside, lit from a common well,
I search for hints of doors inside doors,
A built-in waiting about
Of thresholds and washed floors,
An avid presence demanding flowers and hush.

If I guess right I hope for
A runner of garden, the right length
For taking a prayerbook for a walk,
A small stitching of cemetery ground,
Strict festivals, an hour for the tremble
Of women's laughter, corners for mile-high panics:

And to find the meaning of the women's Christmas.

Peace in the Mountains

The first day I saw this town
I came down the mountain road
Past the old border post, closed now.
The road-signs were in two languages
And the deer were feeding, away
On the far side of the valley,
Pausing and inching forward like photographers.
I slowed and paused and let the car slide forward
Again, the engine off and the gears loose,
Braking and pausing all the way
As far as the first houses and walled gardens.

The wind blew steadily, brushing
Every scrap of paper across the square.
There were rags of many colours
Bundled and packed on the trucks
In the railway siding. A gypsy woman lay
Where she had been struck down beside the bridge.
The ambulance stood by. The money changers
Had closed up their shops for the day.

The same as today, the rushing grey river
Tore downhill past the factory. Somewhere two streets away
It was Saturday and the immigrant weddings were feasted
Behind garden walls with sweet almond milk and loud music.

A Stray

When I heard the voice on the radio
All of a sudden announcing the captives were free
I was holding my young cousin
Forcibly down with two arms
Gripping him back from the street
Where he wanted to flatten himself
Under the wheels of the cars.
I waited for the shot to work
And tried to make out what he had been wearing
Half-recognizing shreds of denim,
An old velvet shirt of my own.

Next week the men were back
Bigger than we remembered
Sitting shakily in the kitchen —
The table a midden of crumbs and documents —
Getting up in the long silences
To carry a cup to the sink
And wash it very carefully.

He stayed upstairs all May.

In June when the raspberries were in
They started to help with the picking
And after that the apples —
They spent days up the ladders
And let us get on with the cooking.
We sat long evenings outside.
But he would not work in the orchard
Or eat with us at meals.

And so it remained, long after
We were used to the loud voices
Hollowing from the fields —
He jumped when he heard them.

You'd find him an odd time smoking
In the courtyard by the bins
At the foot of the steep back stairs

And our liberation never
Reached him. He lived on
Like the last of a whole people
Astray on a lost domain
Bearing all their privations:
No gin and tonic, no
Aspirin, just willow tea.
No tin-openers, no mules, no buses,
No Galician, no Methodists,
No fruit but rotten powdery imploded oranges,
No news from the prison cells.

In Her Other House

In my other house all the books are lined on shelves
And may be taken down in a curious mood.
The postman arrives with letters to all the family,
The table is spread and cleared by invisible hands.

It is the dead who serve us, and I see
My father's glass and the bottle of sour stout at hand
Guarding his place (so I know it cannot be real;
The only boy with six sisters never learned

To set a table, though books lined up at his command).
In this room with a fire, books, a meal and a minute
When everyone is out of sight washing their hands,
A man comes through the door, shedding his coat;

He turns like a dancer before it touches the ground,
Retrieving a lily from somewhere. Where he has been,
You turn out your pockets every time a door is opened;
But the flower has travelled with him and he is in safe
    hands —

On the shelf a letter for him flashes a wide bright stamp.
He mutters once more, *Here goes, in the name of God* —
Women's voices sound outside, he breathes deeply and
    quickly
And returns to talk to the fire, smiling and warming his
    hands —
In this house there is no need to wait for the verdict of
    history
And each page lies open to the version of every other.

In Her Other Ireland

It's a small town. The wind blows past
The dunes, and sands the wide street.
The flagstones are wet, in places thick with glass,
Long claws of scattering light.
The names are lonely, the shutters blank —
No one's around when the wind blows.

The mistress of novices has sent all the novices
Upstairs into the choir to practise
The service for deliverance from storms and thunder.
Their light dapples the sharkskin windows,
The harmonium pants uphill,
The storm plucks riffs on the high tower.

And on the fair green the merry-go-round
Whistles and whirls. The old man has joined
His helper on the plinth. He calls his son
To throw him a rope, and watch for a loosening
Strut or a pelmet or the whole wheel
Spinning lifting and drifting and crashing.

But it spins away, grinding up speed,
Growling above the thunder. The rain
Has begun again; the old man's helper,
Darkfaced with a moustache, holds on.
They try to slow it with their weight,
Calling to the youngster to hang on the rope;

It's a small town, a small town;
Nowhere to go when the wind blows.

The Girl who Married the Reindeer

1

When she came to the finger-post
She turned right and walked as far as the mountains.

Patches of snow lay under the thorny bush
That was blue with sloes. She filled her pockets.
The sloes piled into the hollows of her skirt.
The sunset wind blew cold against her belly
And light shrank between the branches
While her feet shifted, bare,
While her hands raked in the hard fruit.

The reindeer halted before her and claimed the sloes.
She rode home on his back without speaking,
Holding her rolled-up skirt,
Her free hand grasping the wide antlers
To keep her steady on the long ride.

2

Thirteen months after she left home
She travelled hunched on the deck of a trader
Southwards to her sister's wedding.

Her eyes reflected acres of snow,
Her breasts were large from suckling,
There was salt in her hair.

They met her staggering on the quay;
They put her in a scented bath,
Found a silk dress, combed her hair out.

How could they let her go back to stay
In that cold house with that strange beast?
So the old queen said, the bridegroom's mother.

They slipped a powder in her drink,
So she forgot her child, her friend,
The snow and the sloe gin.

3

The reindeer died when his child was ten years old.
Naked in death his body was a man's,
Young, with an old man's face and scored with grief.

When the old woman felt his curse she sickened,
She lay in her tower bedroom and could not speak.
The young woman who had nursed her grandchildren
    nursed her.

In her witch time she could not loose her spells
Or the spells of time, though she groaned for power.
The nurse went downstairs to sit in the sun. She slept.
The child from the north was heard at the gate.

4

Led by the migrating swallows
The boy from the north stood in the archway
That looked into the courtyard where water fell,
His arm around the neck of his companion —
A wild reindeer staggered by sunlight.
His hair was bleached, his skin blistered.
He saw the woman in wide silk trousers

Come out of the door at the foot of the stair,
Sit on a cushion, and stretch her right hand for a hammer.
She hammered the dried broad beans one by one,
While the swallows timed her, swinging side to side:
The hard skin fell away, and the left hand
Tossed the bean into the big brass pot.
It would surely take her all day to do them all.
Her face did not change though she saw the child watching.

A light wind fled over them
As the witch died in the high tower.
She knew her child in that moment:
His body poured into her vision
Like a snake pouring over the ground,
Like a double-mouthed fountain of two nymphs,
The light groove scored on his chest
Like the meeting of two tidal roads, two oceans.

Translation

for the reburial of the Magdalenes

The soil frayed and sifted evens the score —
There are women here from every county,
Just as there were in the laundry.

White light blinded and bleached out
The high relief of a glance, where steam danced
Around stone drains and giggled and slipped across water.

Assist them now, ridges under the veil, shifting,
Searching for their parents, their names,
The edges of words grinding against nature,

As if, when water sank between the rotten teeth
Of soap, and every grasp seemed melted, one voice
Had begun, rising above the shuffle and hum

Until every pocket in her skull blared with the note —
Allow us now to hear it, sharp as an infant's cry
While the grass takes root, while the steam rises:

   Washed clean of idiom · the baked crust
   Of words that made my temporary name ·
   A parasite that grew in me · that spell
   Lifted · I lie in earth sifted to dust ·
   Let the bunched keys I bore slacken and fall ·
   I rise and forget · a cloud over my time.

Bessboro

This is what I inherit —
It was never my own life,
But a house's name I heard
And others heard as warning
Of what might happen a girl
Daring and caught by ill-luck:
A fragment of desolate
Fact, a hammer-note of fear —

But I never saw the place.
Now that I stand at the gate
And that time is so long gone
It is their absence that rains,
That stabs right into the seams
Of my big coat, settling
On my shoulder, in pointed
Needles, crowding the short day.

The white barred gate is closed,
The white fence tracks out of sight
Where the avenue goes, rain
Veils distance, dimming all sound,
And a halfdrawn lace of mist
Hides elements of the known:
Gables and high blind windows.
The story has moved away.

The rain darns into the grass,
Blown over the tidal lough
Past the isolated roof
And the tall trees in the park;
It gusts off to south and west;
Earth is secret as ever:
The blood that was sown here flowered
And all the seeds blew away.

Jesse

As you lie in sleep there grows like a lung inflating
A tree out of your navel, enlarging and toppling
Into its perfection when the leaves and the fruit are soft as air,
Are drenched like capillaries, and as they swell
They become transparent and fade away:

The true tree of knowledge which is good for nothing
But to grow out of your navel like a family tree
That each son and daughter carries the seed of,
That will grow some time and flourish and be gone.

They are able to give you only the light that passes through
    the leaves,
No lasting fruit at all.

Troubler

Did she know what she was at
When she slipped past the garden door
To palm the rolled notes from the teapot,

Or later that night when she pasted
The letter at the back of Hall's *Algebra*
And pierced the date with a needle?

So quickly the instant slid back
In the haystack, pressed by its fellows —
She spent the rest of the evening

Grinning on a sofa by the hour.
The photographs show her all flounces,
Engrossed, a glass in her hand,

But the others' eyes are like foxes' in torchlight;
She surely knew what she was starting: a ruffle
That probed like wind in a northern garden.

In her dreams it's not that she recalls them
But they come, the treasures of time
Lying packed like a knife in a garter

Or scattered among the leaves.
She hears the notes whistled on the half-landing
Just as the sweeping hand crowds the hour.

From an Apparition

Where did I see her, through
Which break in the cloud, the woman
In profile, a great eye like a scared horse?

Seated at a till, her right hand moving,
The fingers landing precisely as if
They stopped notes on a lute, it seemed

That her other hand protected something fragile.
Then she half sprang to her feet, a captive warding off,
And the long swathe of silk she wore began to shift

Flowing away like dye in water, but still she stood
Cramped, and the sliding web lapped against the window
So I knew I was looking at a window,

The silk text building against the glass
In flaps and folds of yellow and arctic blue,
And bottle-dark green until the pane darkened
And closed like a big fringed eyelid into sleep.

The Crevasse

He lay plunged in the funnel of a beanbag,
The glass in his hand as deep as a fjord.
The other went out to answer the telephone,

Leaving both doors open so he could see
A left leg, a left arm and half a ribcage
But no hand. On the far wall, glazed and framed,

A right shoulder and arm crushing flowers
Against a breast. He reached for the bottle again,
And all the vertical lines of the house moved

A little forward, and left. They dangled and waltzed,
Hanging brittle, ready to crash and split
Every straight chair in the room, leaving the halves

To hop away two-legged, leaving
The walls of the house wedged open
To the four winds and the polar light.

An Alcove

What is it, in the air or the walls
Hunched over me, defending
Four stiffbacked chairs caught off guard,
The knitting cramped in its bag
On the low shelf by the dead fire?
The stray cat's tail twitches on the windowsill,
The garden is a patch of frozen grass.

In these rooms every stitch, step and
Edge of a tile is the same age, is wearing
Away at the same rate, like an old lady
Who brings out the sherry because tea means trouble
But has not barred her door.

There are porched crannies, for waiting in while the doctor is
    with her,
And the kind of book one reads in such emergencies,
With mauve and brown pictures, Paolo and Francesca
Coiled like the wisteria's double trunk
In the one safe place, an alcove in the wind.

Autun

As I drove away from the sepulchre of Lazarus,
while the French cows looked sadly out
under the wet branches of Berry,
I could hear other voices drowning
the Grande Polonaise on the radio:

Remember us, we have travelled as far
as Lazarus to Autun,
and have not we too been dead and in the grave
many times now, how long at a stretch
have we had no music but the skeleton tune
the bones make humming, the knuckles warning each other
to wait for the pause and then the long low note
the second and third fingers of the left hand
hold down like a headstone.

How often was I taken apart,
the ribs opened like a liquor press,
and for decades I heard nothing from my shoulders —
my hair flying, at large like a comet —
how often reconstructed,
wrapped and lagged in my flesh, and again
mapped and logged, rolled up and put away
safely, for ever.

On the mornings of my risings
I can hardly see in the steam.
But I know I arise like the infant
that dances out of the womb
bursting with script,
the copious long lines,
the redundant questions of childhood.

She fills the ground and the sky
with ranked and shaken banners,
the scrolls of her nativity.
I stammer out music that echoes like hammers.

Crossing the Loire

I saluted the famous river as I do every year
Turning south as if the plough steered,
Kicking, at the start of a new furrow, my back
To the shady purple gardens with benches under plum trees
By the river that hunts between piers and sandbanks —

I began threading the long bridge, I bowed my head
And lifted my hands from the wheel for an instant of trust,
I faced the long rows of vines curving up the hillside
Lightly like feathers, and longer than the swallow's flight,
My road already traced before me in a dance

Of three nights and three days,
Of sidestepping hills and crescent lights blinding me
(If there was just a bar counter and ice and a glass, and a
    room upstairs:
But it rushed past me and how many early starts before
The morning when the looped passes descend to the ruined
    arch?)

She came rising up out of the water, her eyes were like
    sandbanks
The wrinkles in her forehead were like the flaws in the mist
(Maybe a long narrow boat with a man lying down
And a rod and line like a frond of hair dipping in the stream)
She was humming the song about the estuary, and the
    delights
Of the salt ocean, the lighthouse like a summons; and she
    told me:

The land will not go to that measure, it lasts, you'll see
How the earth widens and mountains are empty, only
With tracks that search and dip, from here to the city of Rome
Where the road gallops up to the dome as big as the sun.

You will see your sister going ahead of you
And she will not need to rest, but you must lie
In the dry air of your hotel where the traffic grinds before
    dawn,
The cello changing gear at the foot of the long hill,

And think of the story of the suitors on horseback
Getting ready to trample up the mountain of glass.

After Leopardi's Storm

The sky clears, and at the top of the street
I can hear the hen giving out her litany,
The stream rattling down the slope
In its tunnel of broom.
                                   The lacemaker now
Stands at her window singing,
Her hand clutching her work, a cloudy ruffle
Wavering its fins in the watery breeze.

Her pale face like the sky
Slowly fills up with light, and spokes of light
Burst from the deep hooded clump of thunder, departing.

Reflected light lies about everywhere.
Like birds we approach, to sip and splash
At the edges of our watery nature, no more —

An ordinary festival that cannot be foreseen
Displays the original spindle
That never came loose, never turned,
But stayed until the long hours wrapped the stem,
Now dark, now bright, an overlapping of wonders
Each one confounding the last.

This afternoon salvation claims
Our whole attention, like grief,
Entirely here, on this side of the mountain
Where the single life is lived, the backbone
Upright, bracing for the next surprise.

Tower of Storms, Island of Tides

The founder of the lighthouse is not here.
She walks through other streets, pausing at a café
To smoke a cigar and check the news and the forecast.

She could not stay for ever in the blinding spray
Watching the sailors being blown on to the rocks,
Listening to the rain like a long thrill on the snare:

She paid for the pilot and the camera that photographed
The bones hanging on the cliff face on the one day of the year
That catches them in the northeast light between pleats of mist.

They flew on then to the islands further west
Where sandy shores offered a landing-place:
One sheltered field, an empty house, salt pastures.

To live there would call for another skill, as fine
As judging the set of milk for cheese,
A belief in the wisdom of a long view from one window.

Water came swimming inward as the tide turned.
They saw far off a stranded dog rushing madly around
A dry patch of sand that was getting smaller and smaller.

It dashed off into the water, then back to its island
Which by now had almost disappeared.

The Bend in the Road

This is the place where the child
Felt sick in the car and they pulled over
And waited in the shadow of a house.
A tall tree like a cat's tail waited too.
They opened the windows and breathed
Easily, while nothing moved. Then he was better.

Over twelve years it has become the place
Where you were sick one day on the way to the lake.
You are taller now than us.
The tree is taller, the house is quite covered in
With green creeper, and the bend
In the road is as silent as ever it was on that day.

Piled high, wrapped lightly, like the one cumulus cloud
In a perfect sky, softly packed like the air,
Is all that went on in those years, the absences,
The faces never long absent from thought,
The bodies alive then and the airy space they took up
When we saw them wrapped and sealed by sickness
Guessing the piled weight of sleep
We knew they could not carry for long;
This is the place of their presence: in the tree, in the air.

The Horses of Meaning

Let their hooves print the next bit of the story:
Release them, roughmaned
From the dark stable where
They rolled their dark eyes, shifted and stamped —

Let them out, and follow the sound, a regular clattering
On the cobbles of the yard, a pouring round the corner
Into the big field, a booming canter.

Now see where they rampage,
And whether they are suddenly halted
At the check of the line westward
Where the train passes at dawn —

If they stare at land that looks white in patches
As if it were frayed to bone (the growing light
Will detail as a thickening of small white flowers),
Can this be the end of their flight?
The wind combs their long tails, their stalls are empty.

A Capitulary

Now in my sleep I can hear them beyond the wall,
A chapterhouse growl, gently continuous:
The sound the child heard, waking and dozing again
All the long night she was tucked up in the library
While her father told his story to the chaplain
And then repeated it before the bishop.

She heard his flat accent, always askew
Responding to the Maynooth semitones,
A pause, and then the whisper of the scribe
Sweeping up the Latin like dust before a brush,
Lining up the ablatives, a refined
Countrywoman's hiss, and the neuter scrape of the pen.

I feel the ticking of their voices and remember how
My sister before she was born listened for hours
To my mother practising scales on the cello;
A grumble of thick string, and then climbing
To a high note that lifted
        that lifted its head
                like a seal —
To a high note that lifted its head like a seal in the water.

Inheriting the Books

They've come and made their camp
Within sight, within slingshot range,
A circle of bulked shapes
Dark inside like wagons.
There are fires like open eyes.
I watch the billows of smoke,
The dark patches, hallucinating
Herds and horses.

Who is that in flashing garments
Bowing to the earth over and over,
Is it a woman or a child?
In the wedge of the valley by the stream
What food are they cooking, what names have they
For washing the dead, for the days of the week?

The long rope has landed, the loose siege hemming me.
In whatever time remains, I will not have the strength to
    depart.

At My Aunt Blánaid's Cremation

In the last dark sidechapel
The faces in the dome
Are bending down like nurses
Who lift, and fix, and straighten
The bed that's always waiting,
The last place you'll lie down.

But your face looks away now,
And we on your behalf
Recall how lights and voices
And bottles and wake glasses
Were lined up like the cousins
In a bleached photograph.

We carry this back to the city
Since the past is all we know —
We remember the snake called Patrick,
Warm in his Aran sleeves —
The past keeps warm, although
It knits up all our griefs:
A cold start in our lives.

Agnes Bernelle, 1923-1999

There is no beast I love better than the spider
That makes her own new centre every day
Catching brilliantly the light of autumn,

That judges the depth of the rosemary bush
And the slant of the sun on the brick wall
When she slings her veils and pinnacles.

She crouches on her knife edge, an ideogram combining
The word for *tools* with the word for *discipline*,
Ready for a lifetime of cold rehearsals;

Her presence is the syllable on the white wall,
The hooked shadow. Her children are everywhere,
Her strands as long as the railway-line in the desert

That shines one instant and the next is doused in dust.
If she could only sing she would be perfect, but
In everything else she reminds me of you.

Borders

for John McCarter

I am driving north to your wake, without a free hand.
I must start at the start, at the white page in my mind.
I no longer own a ribbed corset of rhymes;
I am the witch who stands one-legged, masking one eye.

Passed under the soldier's lenses at Aughnacloy,
I remember how often you crossed the map in a toil
Of love (like Lir's daughter driven to the Sea of Moyle
By spells) from Dublin to Portadown or Armagh to
   Donegal.

So I leap over lines that are set here to hold and plan
The great global waistline in sober monoglot bands,
I follow the road that follows the lie of the land,
Crossing a stream called *Fairy Water*, to come to the bridge
   at Strabane.

A Wave

When is the wave's return?
Everything is still now,
The surface is tight and crawling.

It moves as it is drawn by the future tense
Muttering like a crowd with a rumour of quarrels,
Piled over a reef of glossaries.

Withdrawing it hauled away pebbles, hammering, dumping
On open mouths, boulders flattening words.
So the words are there, but stopped. When the wave comes
    back

Drowning the watchman's brazier.
And the macaronic street cries,
It will flow over all the names.

Words will be there but already,
Written in the new cursive,
They waver like flourishes at the edge of a tide,

A repeating film and ripple,
Clear like thin ice, displaying
A precious mosaic of sand.

The weights are buried,
The cobbles of the woodyard
Sunk with their splinters deep as ballast.

The voice of the wave will be all
We will be expected to understand.

Gloss/Clós/Glas

Look at the scholar, he has still not gone to bed,
Raking the dictionaries, darting at locked presses,
Hunting for keys. He stacks the books to his oxter,
Walks across the room as stiff as a shelf.

His nightwork, to make the price of his release:
Two words, as opposite as *his* and *hers*
Which yet must be as close
As the word *clós* to its meaning in a Scots courtyard
Close to the spailpín ships, or as close as the note
On the uilleann pipe to the same note on the fiddle —
As close as the grain in the polished wood, as the finger
Bitten by the string, as the hairs of the bow
Bent by the repeated note —
                            Two words
Closer to the bone than the words I was so proud of,
Embrace and *strict* to describe the twining of bone and flesh.

The rags of language are streaming like weathervanes,
Like weeds in water they turn with the tide, as he turns
Back and forth the looking-glass pages, the words
Pouring and slippery like the silk thighs of the tomcat
Pouring through the slit in the fence, lightly,
Until he reaches the language that has no word for *his*,
No word for *hers*, and is brought up sudden
Like a boy in a story faced with a small locked door.
Who is that he can hear panting on the other side?
The steam of her breath is turning the locked lock green.

CODA

Kilcash

from the Irish, c. 1800

What will we do now for timber
With the last of the woods laid low —
No word of Kilcash nor its household,
Their bell is silenced now,
Where the lady lived with such honour,
No woman so heaped with praise,
Earls came across oceans to see her
And heard the sweet words of Mass.

It's the cause of my long affliction
To see your neat gates knocked down,
The long walks affording no shade now
And the avenue overgrown,
The fine house that kept out the weather,
Its people depressed and tamed;
And their names with the faithful departed,
The Bishop and Lady Iveagh!

The geese and the ducks' commotion,
The eagle's shout, are no more,
The roar of the bees gone silent,
Their wax and their honey store
Deserted. Now at evening
The musical birds are stilled
And the cuckoo is dumb in the treetops
That sang lullaby to the world.

Even the deer and the hunters
That follow the mountain way
Look down upon us with pity,
The house that was famed in its day;

The smooth wide lawn is all broken,
No shelter from wind and rain;
The paddock has turned to a dairy
Where the fine creatures grazed.

Mist hangs low on the branches
No sunlight can sweep aside,
Darkness falls among daylight
And the streams are all run dry;
No hazel, no holly or berry,
Bare naked rocks and cold;
The forest park is leafless
And all the game gone wild.

And now the worst of our troubles:
She has followed the prince of the Gaels —
He has borne off the gentle maiden,
Summoned to France and to Spain.
Her company laments her
That she fed with silver and gold:
One who never preyed on the people
But was the poor souls' friend.

My prayer to Mary and Jesus
She may come safe home to us here
To dancing and rejoicing
To fiddling and bonfire
That our ancestors' house will rise up,
Kilcash built up anew
And from now to the end of the story
May it never again be laid low.

Hunger

after Langland, Piers Plowman, *Passus VI, 154-303*

When Piers the pilgrim went to the plough
In hope of the harvest of his half-acre
Some workers came willingly to dig and ditch.

. . . But Waster reared up and would have words with him:
Go and piss with your plough, you pennypinching
   preacher —
We'll not starve to please you, we'll steal if we have to,
Your bread and your beef, and we'll live in spite of you.
I never worked, said Waster, and I won't start now,
And I don't give a fiddler's fart for the law
Or for Piers or his party or his plough at all.
Devil mend you, said Piers, I'll do for you all now,
And he hallooed for Hunger who heard him at once:
Show these louts for me they can't lounge for ever.

   Hunger bound Waster about the belly,
He shrank his stomach until his eyes stared,
He battered the boasters about the cheeks
So they looked lanternjawed all their lives after,
He beat them down till their guts were bursting.
Then Piers with half a loaf called Halt! to Hunger.
Let them live he said, and eat with the hogs,
Or have beans and bran broken up together.

   At wind of that word they were away to the haggard,
They threshed his corn till the night threatened,
So Hunger was squinting to have a sight of them,
All for a pot of pea soup Piers had made.
The clergy kilted up the skirts of their habits,
Went out working with spades and shovels,
They dug, they ditched to drive away Hunger.

The blind and the bedridden were better by thousands,
The lame that lay idle were suddenly healed.
The dog's dish was dinner for many hungry
And the beggars were busy for a plate of beans,
The poor were pleased with peas for their wages
And eager to obey when Piers gave the order.

So Piers was proud and put them on his payroll,
Gave wages for their work as he saw them worthy.
Then Piers had pity and bade Hunger go packing,
Go back to his own place and stay there for good —
But whisper, he said first, how shall I handle them?
They'll do what I say as long as they're starving
And they are my brothers, bought with Christ's blood.
Truth once told me to treat them with love —
But if they won't work how am I to have my way?

Hear now, said Hunger, and hold it for wisdom:
Big bold beggars that could work for their bread,
Feed them hens' food and horses' food to help their courage.
Baffle them with beans when their bellies rumble
And if they complain call them to work.
As for the deserving cast down by disaster
Or foundered by fraud, let them find your charity
For the love of Christ and the law of nature,
Alter alterius onera portate
Let each one bear the burden of his brother.
The needy and the naked your goods should nourish;
If you wish for grace follow the Gospel:
Facite vobis amicos de mammona iniquitatis
Let money and Mammon make you friends of the poor.

I would not grieve God, said Piers, for all the earth's
    goods.
May I do as you say without sin? he said then.

Yes surely, said Hunger, unless the Scripture lies.
Go to Genesis, the giant that engendered us all:
In sudore et labore shalt thou earn thy bread,
And *Sapientia* says the same, I saw it in the Bible,
Piger pro frigore would not till his field
And by that he shall beg and none abate his hunger;
And Matthew with the man's face mouths the same story,
The tale of the talents that must be traded
And the moral that was meant when the lord made
    judgement:
He that hath shall have, and help where it's needed,
And he that hath naught shall have naught and get no help
And even what he hopes to have shall be taken from him.

Well, said Piers, tell me something else,
Do you have any little learning in leechcraft?
My company and myself have a curious complaint,
We're in bed all the week with an aching belly.
I know surely, says Hunger, what your sickness is,
Too long at the table makes you groan and grouch.
Take no food until Hunger tells you,
Arise before Appetite has eaten all his fill;
Let this be your diet, I dare venture my ears
Doctor Physic may sell his furred hood for food.

By St Paul, said Piers, I'll profit by your words.
Leave us now Hunger when you like, and adieu.

By God, said Hunger, I've no notion of going
Until I have dined and drunk in your house.

I have no money, said Piers, to buy meat,
I have two fresh cheeses and some curds and cream,
Two bran loaves baked with beans, no bacon,
Parsley and carrots and scallions in my garden.

I've a cow and her calf and a cart mare
To draw dung to my field while the drought lasts;
That's all we have to live on till the day of Lughnasa,
And then I hope to bring home the harvest
When I can design your dinner with the dearest.

    All the poor people fetched in peapods,
Beans and baked apples they brought in their laps,
Chives and chervil and plenty of ripe cherries,
A present to Piers to pay off Hunger,
And Hunger ate in haste and howled for more —
The poor folk for fear fed Hunger fast,
With green roots and peas to poison him they planned —
But now harvest was near, new corn was come home,
They rejoiced and fed Hunger the finest of food
And good ale as Glutton hinted, and bade their guest sleep.

Acknowledgements

Acknowledgements are due to *Continente Irlanda: Storia e scritture contemporanee* (ed. Carla de Petris and Maria Stella, Rome, 2001), *Cyphers, Éire-Ireland, Metre, Princeton University Library Chronicle, The Recorder, R.O.P.E.S., The Southern Review, 13th Moon, Tracks* and *Verse* where some of these poems appeared.

'After Leopardi's Storm' was written for *Or Volge l'Anno: At the Year's Turning*, edited by Marco Sonzogni (Dedalus, Dublin, 1998).

'To the Angel in the Stone' was written to be carved on a stone outside Salisbury Cathedral for the Salisbury Festival, 1999, and was published in *Last Words: New Poetry for the New Century*, edited by Don Paterson and Jo Shapcott (Picador, London, 1999).

An earlier version of 'A Wave' was written for a book produced for the Ulster Museum.

An earlier version of 'In Her Other House' was published in *Odes to the Future*, a privately published Festschrift for Pearse Hutchinson.

'Inheriting the Books' appeared in *25*, produced for a reading in the Abbey Theatre, Dublin, to mark twenty-five years of The Gallery Press.

'Kilcash' was translated for *Kilcash: A History, 1190-1801*, by John Flood and Phil Flood (Geography Publications, Dublin, 1999).